SCHIRMER'S LIBRARY
OF MUSICAL CLASSICS

Vol. 752

FRIEDRICH BURGMÜLLER

Op. 109

Eighteen Characteristic Studies

(Etudes de Genre)

For the Piano

A Sequel to the Studies, Op. 100

Dedicated to

STEPHEN HELLER

Edited and Fingered by

LOUIS OESTERLE

G. SCHIRMER, *Inc.*

DISTRIBUTED BY

7777 W. BLUEMOUND RD. P.O. BOX 13819 MILWAUKEE, WI 53213

Eighteen
Characteristic Studies.

Confidence.

F. BURGMÜLLER. Op. 109, Book I.

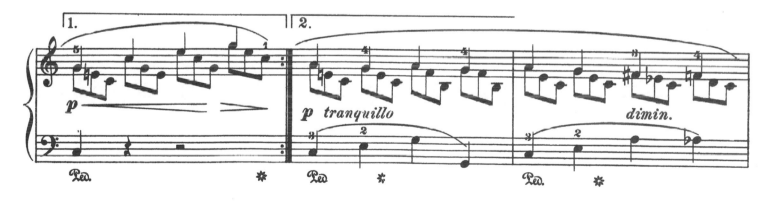

Les Perles.
The Pearls.

Le Retour du Pâtre.

The Shepherd's Return.

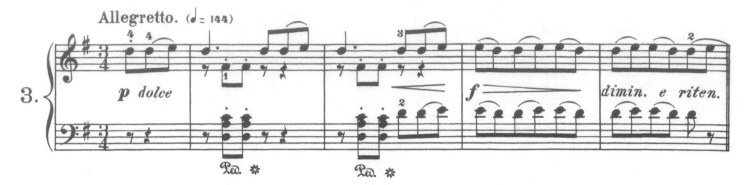

Les Bohémiens

The Gypsies.

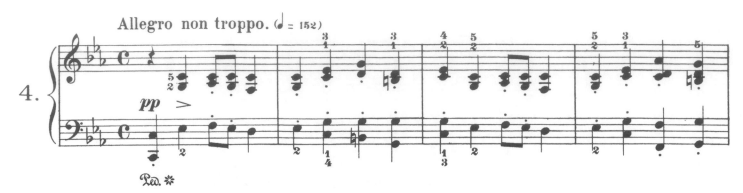

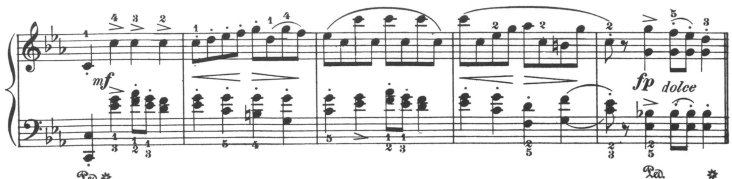

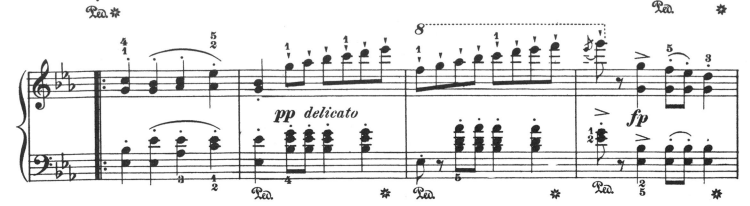

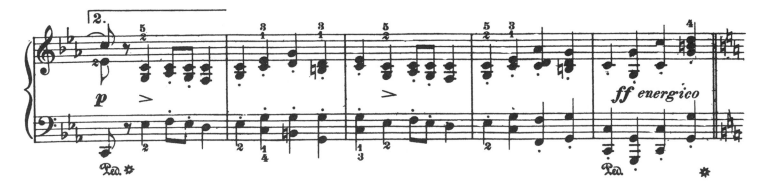

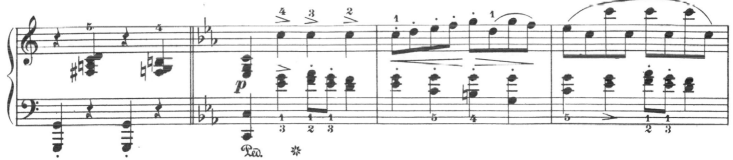

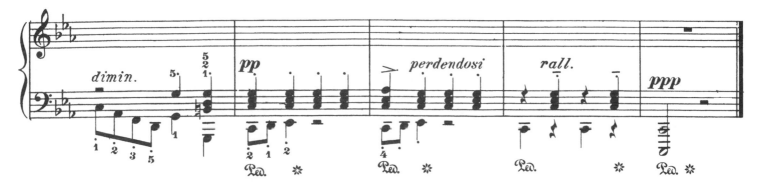

La Source.
The Spring.

L'enjouée.
Light-hearted Maiden.

Berceuse.
Lullaby.

Agitato.

La Cloche des Matines.
Matin Bell.

Eighteen
Characteristic Studies.

La Vélocité.
Velocity.

F. BURGMÜLLER. Op. 109. Book II.

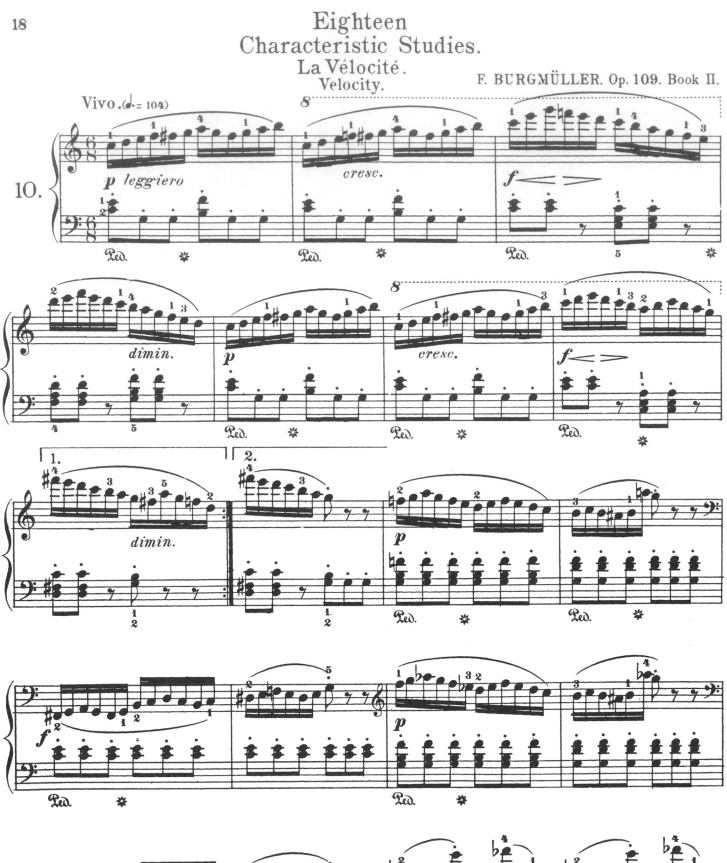

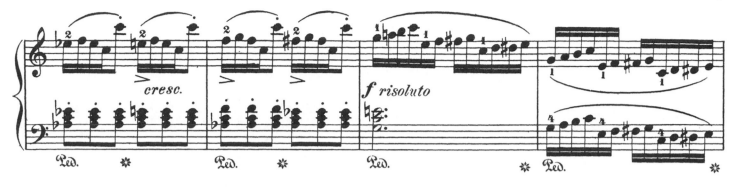

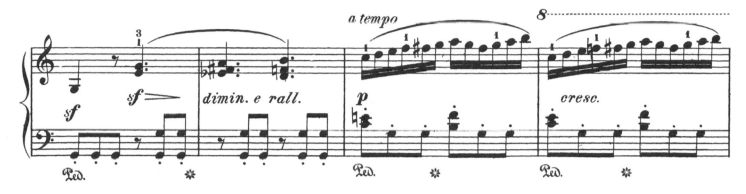

La Sérénade.

Serenade.

Allegretto grazioso. (♪ = 176.)

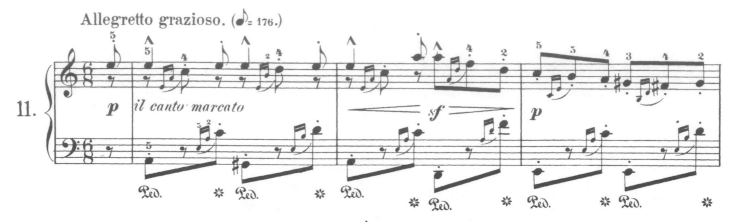

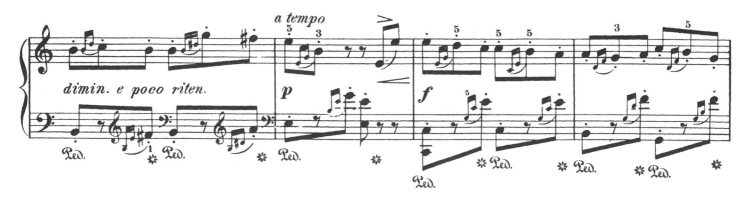

Le Réveil dans les Bois.
Awakening in the Wood.

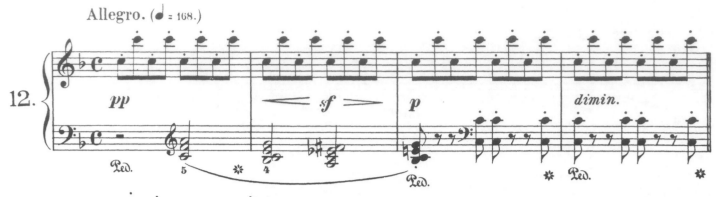

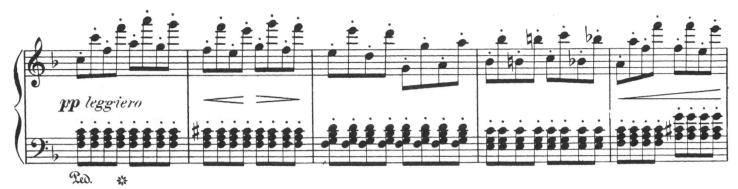

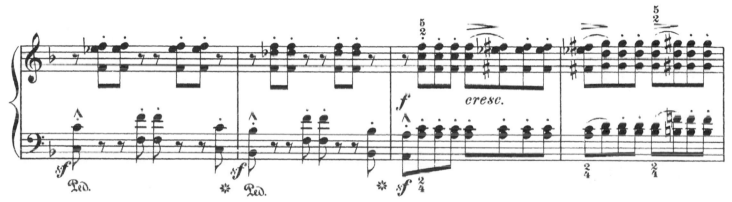

L'Orage.
The Storm.

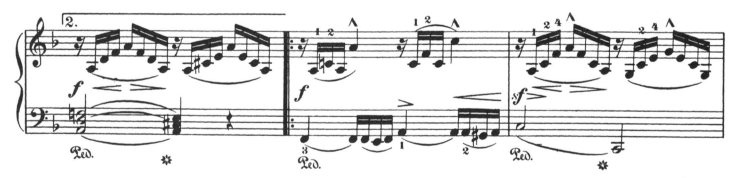

This étude may serve as an introduction to the next.

Refrain du Gondolier.
Lay of the Gondolier.

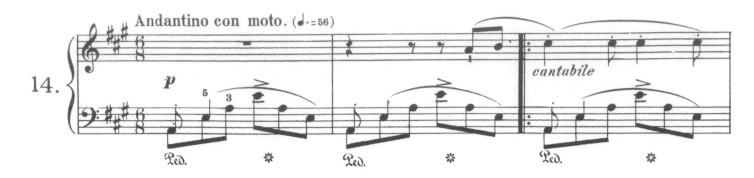

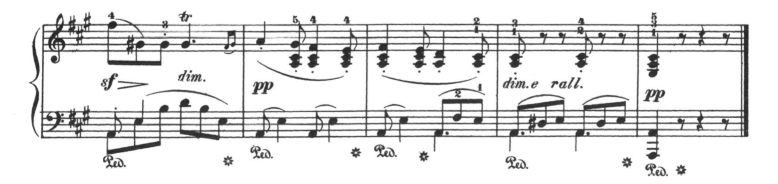

Les Sylphes.
Sylphs.

15.

La Séparation.
Parting.

Allegro agitato. (♩=152)

16.

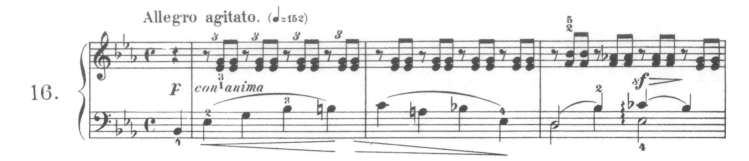

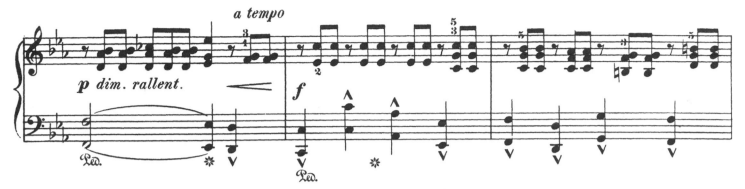

La Marche.
March.

17.

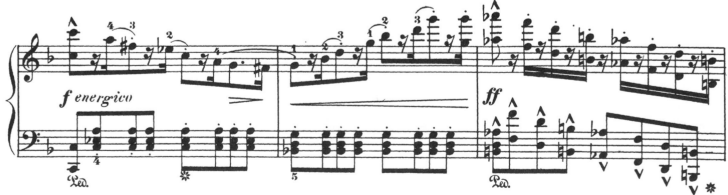

La Fileuse.
At the Spinningwheel.

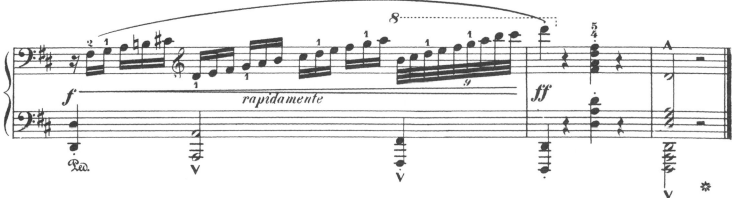